Praise for *Sixty Sonnets*

Ernest Hilbert's sure-footed poems have the breathless urgency of a man telling others the way out of a burning building. Unafraid to startle, often winning out over recalcitrant material, they score astonishing successes. A bold explorer with few rivals, Hilbert enlarges the territory of traditional form. *Sixty Sonnets* may be the most arresting sequence we have had since John Berryman checked out of America.

> —X.J. Kennedy, author of *Lords of Misrule*
> and editor of *Literature: An Introduction to Fiction, Poetry, and Drama*

Hilbert has an appetite for life equal to his taste in literature: a rare combination in an age of dissociated sensibility. In these sonnets, whose dark harmonies and omnivorous intellect remind the reader of Robert Lowell's, Hilbert is alternately fugitive and connoisseur, hard drinker and high thinker. But he is always a true poet, proud to belong to the company of those who still feel "The last, noble pull of old ways restored, / Valued and unwanted, admired and ignored."

> —Adam Kirsch, author of
> *The Modern Element: Essays on Contemporary Poetry*

For scale alone, the project at first seems improbable. But then you read, and it's clear that Hilbert's sensibility, bright-hued and gothic, sentimental, precise and ambitious, could be contained by no less. These wry and lovely poems are for anyone whose curiosity ranges from Petrarch to improv, and the result is a complex portrait of the America of our current era—composed in singing verse!

> —Dave King, Rome Prize-winning author of the novel *The Ha-Ha*

More Praise for *Sixty Sonnets*

Just as the work of the modernists showed that the best free verse usually has something masterfully formal about it, Hilbert's fine collection might serve to remind us that the best formal poetry has about it a marvelous colloquial freshness and inventiveness, and the ring of an actual human voice. It is a touching and intelligent book.

— Franz Wright, recipient of the Pulitzer Prize for Poetry

Sixty Sonnets delights in a decidedly badass bravura. Hilbert's red-blooded diction and febrile subjects put paid to any lingering suspicions about traditional verse's chronic anemia. His erudition is salted with humor, his romantic flights with a rage for order. He is a twenty-first century beatnik in Elizabethan ruff. A smashing debut!

— David Yezzi, author of *The Hidden Model*

The American lyric rendered in these poems follows Coleridge's description of the sonnet as "adapted to the state of a man violently agitated by a real passion." Hilbert's passion here is to contain, precious piece by precious piece, the unordinary quotidian of the American poetic. *Sixty Sonnets* is a gift to all of us from an exceptional ear and a fine consciousness.

— Afaa Michael Weaver, author of *Multitudes*

Sixty Sonnets

Sixty Sonnets

Ernest Hilbert

 RED HEN PRESS | *Los Angeles, California*

Sixty Sonnets
Copyright © 2009, 2019 by Ernest Hilbert
All rights reserved

Design and layout by Sydney Nichols

ISBN: 978-1-59709-361-3
Library of Congress Catalog Card Number: 2008940274

No grants or fellowships were disturbed in the composition of these poems.

The City of Los Angeles Department of Cultural Affairs, Los Angeles County Arts Commission, California Arts Council and the National Endowment for the Arts partially support Red Hen Press.

First Edition
Published by Red Hen Press
www.redhen.org

Acknowledgements

I extend gratitude to the editors of the magazines and newspapers in which these poems originally appeared, including *The New Republic, American Poetry Review, New York Sun, American Literary Review, Poetry East, Georgetown Review, Cimarron Review, Pleiades: A Journal of New Writing, The New Criterion, Unpleasant Event Schedule, Vocabula Review, Perihelion, Del Sol Review, Ducts,* and *Revolting Sofas.*

"Prophetic Outlook," "Domestic Situation," "Fortunate Ones," "White Noise," "The Singles Scene," and "Love Poem" appeared on the *Best American Poetry* website. "Domestic Situation," "Magnificent Frigatebird," "Mirage," "Church Street," "Fortunate Ones," and "In Bed for a Week" appeared in *The Swallow Anthology of New American Poets*, Ohio University Press, 2009. Early and final versions of "Magnificent Frigatebird" appeared in an essay prepared for the book *Poem, Revised*, Marion Street Press, 2008. "Gold Rush (On Disposing of an Old Sofa)," "The Singles Scene," and "AAA Vacation Guide" appeared in the comic book *Gold Rush* by Robert Algeo, In Abstentia Press, 2009. "Epitaphs" appeared as the mini-comic *Epitaphs* by Robert Algeo, In Absentia Press, 2009. Twelve of the poems in this collection will appear in recorded form on the album *Legendary Misbehavior*, Pub Can Records, 2009. "Love Poem" was set to music by composer Daniel Felsenfeld.

Many thanks to Daniel Felsenfeld, Kate Gale, Jennifer Mercer, Niamh O'Connell, Jessica Caum, Kara Mallon, Melissa Moffa, Andrew Hallman, Natalie and David Bauman, and all my friends and family. Special thanks to my dry cleaner, who got the blood out of my white cotton shirt. I would also like to thank friends whose sharp and sensible comments proved indispensable, most especially Andrew Goodspeed, without whom this book could not have found its final form.

For Lynn

Table of Contents

FAILED ESCAPES

On the Twenty-fifth Anniversary of John Lennon's Murder ... 21

Corned Beef Hash and Two Eggs Over Easy, Coffee ... 22

William James Still, Drowned in the Delaware River ... 23

Fight or Flight ... 24

She Remembers How They Fled from
the Liquor Store Robbery in New Mexico ... 25

The Fugitive Spends Christmas in a Las Cruces Motel Room ... 26

EXAMINATIONS AND CONCLUSIONS

Poem Begun on the Autumn Equinox ... 29

Magnificent Frigatebird ... 30

Photographs above the Desk (*Amphisbaenics*) ... 31

Genealogies ... 32

Mirage ... 33

History   34

A Suburbanite Briefs a Historian   35

The Pessimist Prepares for What May Well Be His Last Winter   36

The Retired Literary Critic Pauses in His Sunday Reading   37

White Noise   38

Dear Plato   39

Tourist Economy   40

LEGENDARY MISBEHAVIOR

Church Street   43

A Few Drinks and We're All Poets   44

Cautionary Tale; or, What Goes Up Must Come Down   45

Up Late on a Work Night: A Lament   46

Coil   47

Improprieties   48

Blotter   49

Domestic Situation   50

A Sad Last Number for the Gentlemen at the Tavern   51

SATIRES AND OBSERVATIONS

Fortunate Ones	55
The Singles Scene	56
Prophetic Outlook	57
His Secret Foe: Gravity	58
AAA Vacation Guide	59
"Thou Shalt Commit Adultery"	60
Reality TV	61
Andromeda Chained to the Rock	62
Gold Rush (On Disposing of an Old Sofa)	63
Epitaphs	64
She Discovers an Unsent E-Mail to an Ex-Boyfriend	65
Guide to the Modern Man (*Beach Issue!*)	66
The Otherwise Sedentary Novelist Finds His Fantasy Turns Out All Wrong	67
The King Issues His Annual Report	68

SMALL CONSOLATIONS

Song   71

Symmetries   72

Letter to a Godson   73

Love Poem   74

LITERATURE AND RELATED EMBARRASSMENTS

Meet and Greet   77

Literary Artifacts   78

Leander Without Heroes   79

Rules of Order   80

In the Arena   81

Decisive Victories   82

The War Correspondent Returns to His Neighborhood   83

Thoughts upon Reading George Gissing's *New Grub Street*   84

Elegies and Laments

At the Grave of Thomas Eakins, Late Winter   87

Biglin Brothers Racing   88

The Ancient Sailor Leaves
  His Heartless Patrician Lover to Her Lyre   89

Nightmare   90

Lines on the Winter Solstice   91

In Bed for a Week   92

Calavera for a Friend   93

Facilis descensus Averni

Failed Escapes

It's not dark yet, but it's getting there.

—*Bob Dylan*

On the Twenty-fifth Anniversary of John Lennon's Murder

On a step behind the Holiday Inn,
Two Russians roamed up, bummed a cigarette,
While a third snuck up, struck me from behind.
I sprawled to asphalt. Then the boot came in.
I swung through the red, but it's a good bet
I didn't land one. The blackout was kind.
I woke knotted in blood-ruined sheets, startled:
Smashed, stamped, and splintered to a numbed dazzle,
I spat black wads into the fuzzy sink.
One look in the mirror, my brain curdled.
I propped in the shower stall. Steam sizzled.
My hair loosened a sick swirl of sour pink.
They made off, grinning, with all I had: two
Dollars, five cigarettes, and my Zippo.

Corned Beef Hash and Two Eggs Over Easy, Coffee

I'm battered all to hell. You should see me.

I'm in the corner of a bright diner,

The very one from Suzanne Vega's song.

Every time I limp to the john to pee

The whole crowd stares at my glaring shiner.

My whole face: swollen eggplant. Before long

I will try to remember what happened.

Memory is just a haunting of ghosts,

And the night is crushed below like eggshell.

In the ER the doctors pretended

I would be fine, and they were quite good hosts.

They stapled my head back together well.

I am sinking on a soft black balloon,

Dreaming of the break. It is coming soon.

William James Still, Drowned in the Delaware River

October 23rd, 1898, Gloucester County

When I think back so far, light and shape blur,
As the sun-shot leaves above did for you,
Drowned, snug in muck, staring up to the world.
Just as the jokes and leaps on shore spurred
The picnic on, like life, history's glue
Slung you to river bottom, caught and furled.
How long before they paused, and you were missed?
Did noon light waft through the slow green to you?
How long before they began to gather?
The cold edge of the world closed on you, kissed
You shut. To the first searchers, surfaces threw
Back mirrored sky, hid your tortured weather.
The fairgrounds, littered with bunting and trash,
Grew cold also. Great bonfires sank to ash.

Fight or Flight

For a retired boxer

Trekking city streets, I am mercury
Tilting in glints down a vertical grid.
I am as much an Iliadic
As a cool Odyssean entity.
I force my course, and I never could
Flee a fight, however idiotic.
It's easier to run than to stand off,
But then I'd wonder if I could have won
If I had just held my square of sidewalk.
All my flights lead only to further loss.
All victories become added burden.
All escapes and scars may as well be mocked:
Days drizzle to dust, and the cold years creep,
As great oceans gather rain in my sleep.

She Remembers How They Fled from
the Liquor Store Robbery in New Mexico

Unleashed, we sped hard through the sunset rush,
To the west, still fierce like stung animals,
Blood honeyed, making for the dusty sun,
Our future seething to a raw gorgeous crush.
Flaming cloud-runs slowly thawed like candles
On the sad, unattainable horizon.
You'd been shot three times, soaked with tar and sweat,
But you gunned the grimy frame toward night,
Lit a smoke and cringed at the oily guts
Leaking from your side. You could never let
Them win. You winced and gripped my small wrist tight,
As we lurched off the road into dirt ruts,
Launched out to tether's end, high from the pain,
The past dragging and chiming like a chain.

The Fugitive Spends Christmas in a
Las Cruces Motel Room

Stale tamales for breakfast with pale tea,
Cool daybreak fires over the bronzed valley.
Grizzled pink tatters down the jet-flaked blue.
The cruel moon curves and makes chaos of the sea,
Sways around again to drag night from me.
Time has ground me sharp, but I know I'm through.
He's in a mound of stones and chaparral.
We didn't get much cash. It's nearly gone.
Life is gathered closer here, and death too.
I'm sad, and I have no one left to call.
I peek through blinds, sit on the bed alone.
These kind blue pills burn me up and make me new.
I'm wasted and true, savage, coarse, and far.
Winter smoothes me away like an old scar.

Examinations and Conclusions

It is not night, it's just dark.

—Dean Young

Poem Begun on the Autumn Equinox

The graveyard is as orderly and clean
As the playing fields and ballpark nearby.
I park the jeep midway between the two.
I wonder what this short distance can mean.
Partly gone from all that appears early,
At thirty-five I'm at least half way through.
One wine-red leaf sinks through the humid air.
At its end, summer still feels like itself.
Seasons start slowly. They end that way too:
One more check, one more payment, one less hair.
One may still add grains of learning and wealth,
But the mornings that remain seem too few.
There's nothing to hear on the radio.
The river is low, foams white, and runs slow.

Magnificent Frigatebird

The sharp dark thorn plummets like a dive-bomber,
No human moment of hesitation
In its rush through raw wind to join its goal.
Fish gather in quick, silver clouds, swell, veer.
They swim beneath this black-lit beacon,
Long-beaked chevron of darkness, lance of coal,
Swiftly struck ink dash, aiming down hard
Like a stealth fighter, so fast it suffers
No lapse of purpose. Poised and sinister,
Over a glistening sea, the Pirate Bird
Studies the breakers for new kills, hovers—
Earth its vast blank canvas and theater—
Supreme as midday sun, brutal as the sea,
And chosen, death's fond emissary.

Photographs above the Desk (*Amphisbaenics*)

In the photographs, stark portions of time
Are stalled. The poets pose in snow, with pets,
Gripping drinks, arching brows, playing the part.
Possum, perched stiffly, can't help but emit
Grim rays of disapproval. On the step
At Faber, young Hughes rests in the jawed trap
Of Auden and Eliot (the Raja),
Plotting his escape from their gray, regal
Company, and so (under which liar)
We see three whole generations ajar.
So thank God for gin, whiskey, and lager,
Publisher's parties. Let the critics rail.
Too much chat of gyres, grails, gods, Rose, or Rood
Will leave a young man questing for the door.

Genealogies

I envy those who trace their families back
And back, to covered wagons, Bunker Hill,
The Mayflower, and Bayeux Tapestry.
Some can worm all the way down to the Dark
Ages, before which all bets are off. Still,
I know nil of mine and would like to see:
What's back there? What's burrowed in the wood lot,
What turnpikes of genealogy sped
My kin through ages and nations to me?
Two generations back my short file stops.
This slender family branch must have once led
To trunk if not root. What strange folk were we?
Gangsters and seamstresses, what bizarre links,
Smiths and sylphs, deacons and drunks, kings and finks?

Mirage

Once, when I was young, an odd thing occurred.
I found myself in trouble for some stunt,
Some selfish offense forgotten since then.
For a time, my mother's smile was deferred,
And I learned it was something I would want
To get back so I could feel fine again.
For a brief but blurred flash, from the top stair,
I thought she smiled at me. What a relief.
I smiled back, but she scowled. What went wrong?
I grew confused. I was struck, standing there.
What slipped in my reckless reach for reprieve?
I grasped a mirage, unreal as a song.
I was shocked by the sheer drop from assurance,
The vast span that parts us from our parents.

History

We can talk of eras and epochs,
But life smudges over easy margins,
Blows down fences, confuses neat frontiers.
We may witness sunsets and check our clocks,
But authentic change is slow, and it spins
So languidly we lose sight of the years.
My barber is the last of a proud type.
Sinatra grins on the wall. Sopranos
Soar from the radio. He stocks *Playboy*.
My barber, stooped, kindly, will never gripe.
Men's hair will thin and beards will grow. He knows
A thousand jokes, and he fought on D-Day.
He holds the worn rope's end of times far gone,
Frayed to a thread, weighted with songs, and wars we won.

A Suburbanite Briefs a Historian

Oh, Lord, the middle class is so damned dull.
I am sure you have heard this all before,
And so far as I can tell it's largely true.
But it is fun to be so *bourgeois*, full
Of all reliable means and much more
That is deserved once you have paid your due.
We enjoy screens wider than SUVs,
Pools like dots of detergent from the sky,
As sprinklers skitter like crickets on lawns.
But what would you prefer to all of these
Suburbs? We can't ride to hounds or just fly
Off whenever we like to our own islands.
And we can't go back to what came before,
Ten to a room, half sleeping on the floor.

The Pessimist Prepares for
What May Well Be His Last Winter

I have been released into harsh Autumn
And witness ash of cruel light on skylines.
Dusk draws in fast; dawn bears barbarous frost.
The earth, tilting on its axis, will come
To its winter, while I expire in lines.
I pour a short glass, talk of what is lost,
Small thoughts, as pine smoke, leaves tugged loose by wind.
I simmer soups, light candles for the dark,
Swaddle myself in long scarves and jacket.
My heart, besieged at its peak, will not mend.
I set out to visit the empty park,
Breathe fierce evening, stroll one slow circuit.
Autumns return, but I can only spend
My seasons, as small fires, toward my end.

The Retired Literary Critic
Pauses in His Sunday Reading

I still wonder who declined in this room
Before me, in this rented antique house,
As chips of light fleck the blown curtain.
The ceiling's like the lid of a tomb.
Who slept off a drunken soiree or doused
Lice with witch hazel? What trivia passed then?
The May afternoon remains cool and sad.
The bed is old and sunken to the side.
On this crude rostrum, hope is not enough.
I once loved a girl with dark hair. I had
Years to be happy. When did I decide
What was consequential, what was mere stuff?
Late cries rise like lost balloons from the park,
And day sinks into magnifying dark.

White Noise

The past does not fade, nor does it decline;
It merely grows louder, slightly, tone by tone,
Until its vast din is blank as silence.
The grand chords boom on for some time:
Caesar and Charlemagne, Curie, Capone—
Centuries will mute their once crucial sense.
My songs are lost, as all will be at last,
Unremembered as a minor fiefdom,
Its peasants who tilled fields and died in wars.
As we gain the crest, what we lose goes fast.
Goals fray into ragged, rebellious outcomes,
Announced by anonymous ambassadors.
The roar of dates and battles grows louder,
Drowns all who care, and all who do not care.

Dear Plato

When it comes to love and peace, that's it,
We will never really learn to grow up.
Tantrums scorch; jealous, hurtful flares bear light
In the darkness we fashion from splendid
Old grudges. As if bored, we interrupt
Days with insults that keep us up all night.
In the sandbox of suburbs, swing-sets of cities,
We endure and grin, reach for temptations,
Struggle to decide why we are not more pleased
With success or acquisition. We tease
Out some turmoil from order, privations
From abundance; catch only to release:
The way of the human variety,
Not even happy just being happy.

Tourist Economy

Winter mornings douse the bald hills
Of Todos Santos, painted town of All Saints,
Bauble of the Baja, bright tourist trap.
"Hotel California" *muzak* fills
Cafes and cheerful shops, where few complaints
Are heard in opulent aisles of chintzy crap.
Two paved streets, ten thousand chickens, five bars,
Very little to do but drink and read,
Canadians lounge, lunch, and entertain.
Americans cruise idly in sports cars.
Hard to think such distinct wealth does not breed
Some animosity or quiet disdain,
But the townspeople are patient, go to school,
Tend graves, get paid, and try to stay cool.

Legendary Misbehavior

Tempus fuckit.

—*Franz Wright*

I thank the Lord for crudity.

—*Robert Frost*

Church Street

For Daniel Nester

My friends quietly dropped out of high school.
It seemed each week we had parties for some guy
Going into jail or getting released.
It's not that anyone thought this was cool,
Only good wishes that the time would fly,
And after twenty beers he might find some peace.
Now that I look back, with no emotion,
We needed parties. We liked company.
We hardly needed a reason at all:
Never sweet-sixteen or graduation,
But funeral, fresh hitch in the army,
Baby soon for the sad girl in the hall.
We'd vent, catch any reason to not grieve,
Revel down days torn from the years we'd leave.

A Few Drinks and We're All Poets

We'll head out, you and me, have a pint, or
Maybe three, a cool thin ale, like sunlight,
Or a lager, toke the dregs of the day.
We'll catch up, slide down, the barmaid will pour
And we'll lean back from the compulsory fight
Over a highborn lady or new play.
A few shots, icy beaker of thinned gin,
Warm welcome of a good whiskey, and not
One moment to spare, as the bell will have rung.
They will pad you for guns on the way in,
And you'll have a fine time, if you don't get shot.
This is our last stark, sad chance to feel young.
What else to say of our faint star-fall town,
But we've sunk so low, we might as well drown.

Cautionary Tale; or,
What Goes Up Must Come Down

Mushrooms, cocaine, whiskey: go on, get high.

You know it will be a whole lot of fun.

But there are rules, and they will be obeyed.

You've been duly warned, but still you'll ask why

You can't have it all. The longer the run,

The bigger the final bill to be paid.

It's a seesaw, the old scales of justice:

Metaphysics and morals aside,

You'll feel it right down to each toasted cell.

Nature's ancient laws will not be dismissed.

No matter how much you might care to try,

You won't avoid it: It's gravity's pull.

Rise and drop, buzz and stumble, crash and rush,

You can only get away with so much.

Up Late on a Work Night: A Lament

O noctem præclaram!

When his brain is drenched with Chesterfield Ale,
He loves tapping out long, soppy e-mails
To seasoned friends and admired enemies.
While he does this, he listens to a hail
Of lewd noise, and heavy metal prevails.
He lights another, downs more beer with ease.
He could spend his whole life like this, washed out
And glazed over, swimming the molten soup
Of slack, smoky time, beery underwater,
Slow motion slide, the roar of chords, the shout
Of it all, the endless bottle-clunked loop,
The slender filament charred forever:
But bitter ghosts ache through his bones for days.
He grows to regret his asinine ways.

Coil

Is it still alive? Or is it a frame
Bared of its bright canvas, a skeleton
Whose fats, organs, and skin have been boiled off?
A mess of blood and nerve is not the same
As a child sprawled on park grass with the sun
On her skin, liable to laugh, itch, and cough.
A deer, stuffed, is immune to bolt and virus.
It looks real. It's all there. It's got its parts.
But it's dead. What breathed there did not survive.
Light will excite cornea and iris.
Enormous gas clouds will ignite into stars.
Engines, precise and fueled, will roar alive.
One may jam parts in place, but something must
Spark it hard, hurt it; force it from the dust.

Improprieties

For Ffej Prorock

My friend is a fugitive from the law.
For fifteen years he's been on the "run."
What to do? Let's get this cold keg started.
We'll deal with it tomorrow. The one flaw
In the system is just how little fun
It is once it's got you boxed and carded.
Youthful transgressions fester. We still move
Against the commonwealth, however small
Our motions may be. Some guys really do
Get away with murder. Try to improve
On that. Just read the papers. We all fall
From time to time, and will until we're through.
You can only laugh. You will never win,
But, still, it's pointless to turn yourself in.

Blotter

There are some things I never planned to do,
But found myself governed by the moment.
Once, I helped smash a record studio
With a sledgehammer and nail gun, then threw
Buckets of piss out onto the pavement.
That one, I suppose you might as well know.
I helped lift a coffin out of a bar
To a waiting hearse and got a free round.
I ran from cops and actually got away.
I caused some havoc in a stolen car.
I know none of these dumb stunts is new ground,
But they're the few I remember today.
I wound up in jail once, which is no fun.
Sometimes you will hide when you should have run.

Domestic Situation

Maybe you've heard about this. Maybe not.
A man came home and chucked his girlfriend's cat
In the wood chipper. This really happened.
Dinner wasn't ready on time. A lot
Of other little things went wrong. He spat
On her father, who came out when he learned
About it. He also broke her pinky,
Stole her checks, and got her sister pregnant.
But she stood by him, stood strong, through it all,
Because she loved him. She loved him, you see.
She actually said that, and then she went
And married him. She felt some unique call.
Don't try to understand what another
Person means by love. Don't even bother.

A Sad Last Number for the Gentlemen at the Tavern

This one is for all the aging fuck-ups,
The guys who can't get their shit in one bag,
Can't find a job much less get there on time.
They struggle to grind tires out of deep ruts,
But they slide back in. They will always lag
In the long race, skid down while others climb.
There are, as a rule, women, kids, and pets
Who learn not to depend on them so much,
Who go on with their lives, nurse their grudges.
What keeps these men from growing up? What gets
Dropped behind them? Something must make them flinch
From life's harsh contours, its many judges:
As if they prefer to remain children,
More loved, and more easily forgiven.

Satires and Observations

The world has gone mad today,
And good's bad today,
And black's white today,
And day's night today.

—Cole Porter

Fortunate Ones

You will inherit large sums of money
(But someone dear to you will have to die first).
You will travel far and see the wide world
(And load yourself with debt; these things aren't free).
You can relax now. You've been through the worst
(But it consumed your youth, and now you're old).
You will enjoy many warm times with friends
(But they will sneak your booze and filch your smokes).
Your fortune is in some other cookie
(Hard to argue the message that one sends).
You are very important to your folks
(They will never let your life be easy).
A fortune is only worth what it covers
(Believe what you like, discard the others).

The Singles Scene

As a girl, she had an odd assortment
Of dolls, all missing their partners and mates:
Cher with no Sonny, two Charlie's Angels.
Her strange daydreams all centered on absent
Friends, a Ken doll, spiffed up, who never dates,
And a bionic woman who settles
For nights alone; Luke who misses Leia,
Donny who pines for his lost Marie,
While Ace Frehley, with no band, goes solo.
Glinda the Good Witch has been stood up. A
Worthless complement, she's sorry to see
The single wrestler, who never felt so low,
Not worth much without an adversary,
Sad as a graveyard on a summer day.

Prophetic Outlook

Crooks run the whole world, and the Dow just fell.
Crap rules the airwaves. All your best plans stall.
The air is dirty, and you don't feel well.
Your wife won't listen. Friends no longer call.
Sad songs from youth no longer cast a spell.
Cancer research has run into a wall.
Some inflated hack just won the Nobel.
You witness clear signs of decline and fall.
The neighbors are cold, and your house won't sell.
Your cat has bad teeth. Your paychecks feel small.
Maybe you're really sick. It's hard to tell.
Up ahead, traffic has slowed to a crawl.
The world didn't just start going to hell.
You just noticed for the first time, that's all.

His Secret Foe: Gravity

I have a friend who falls off of bar stools.
He'll do it every time. Just watch and *boom*
He's down. The tall chairs at old Astor Lounge,
Downtown, become teetering pedestals;
In noon light or after-hours back room,
If there's some dignity left to scrounge,
He blows it. With a thud he's floored.
The fat vinyl discs crossed with tape strips
In the smoking neon dark of Bellevue
And the greasy sheen of Holland Bar next door
Are Olympic platforms for his choice tricks.
One second he's there, then he's gone from view.
The next day, with puzzling bruises that smart,
He recalls none of this gratifying art.

AAA Vacation Guide

"Philadelphia isn't as bad as Philadelphians say it is."
—*Billboard on Interstate 95*

Paris in the Spring, Autumn in New York,
Singers pair a city with a season
As though it belonged to it all year long.
They should try to put a few more to work:
Trenton in winter needs a good reason;
Scranton in summer seems so very wrong.
How about Cincinnati in the spring?
Autumn in Passaic, or in Oakland?
Some cities just lack glamour and appeal,
And there is no point arguing the thing.
No one reads through stacks of brochures to spend
A honeymoon in Allentown. Let's get real.
Most places on the map, you must believe,
No one wants to visit, only to leave.

"Thou Shalt Commit Adultery"

Exodus, 20:14

Blue pencil and red pen, fix what you can,
But words are like ball bearings or beach sand:
Once out of the pouch, you can't hold them all.
Something always slips through, trips up the plan.
Most typos are harmless. We understand
What's meant. Others spring from the devil.
The 1631 King James has this
Howler: "thou shalt commit adultery."
Really, now. It would become a headache
For a lot of guys, who would rather miss
Out on an affair to stay secretly
Home with their wives. Even if a mistake
By the Word of the law, they would be blessed,
And edit the Book out of sheer laziness.

Reality TV

Gossip often centers on TV shows
Viewers have in common. This is not strange.
What else can be so equal and shared?
Discussions of real estate, everyone knows,
Soon show that some can exist in a range
That surpasses what others ever cared
To know about. Talk of sex will reveal
That someone's not getting any. Talk of
New books won't fly, unless Oprah picked them.
Men have sports, but it serves most to conceal
How unalike they are otherwise. What love
Is squandered in this public fantasy, when
Families watch others choke on worms,
So familiar, now, no one even squirms?

Andromeda Chained to the Rock

Perseus, still on the lam, hoped to rest,
But, of course, he came across an undressed
Virgin, shadowed by a Kraken in the tide.
Hoping to avoid another awkward test
Of his manhood, he sighed and then confessed
That he really didn't want to choose sides:
"Her mom, Cassiopeia, shouldn't she
Be the one out there chained up and soused
With sea spray, to pay for her own blunder?
Still drowsy and cranky—who wouldn't be?—
Lonely Kraken never asked to be roused
By nymphs from his happy, sea-snug slumber."
Kraken agreed: "Just proceed on your way.
Move along. Nothing to see here today."

Gold Rush (On Disposing of an Old Sofa)

What natural or man-made wonders will we
Prospect in those crevasses and gullies,
Boulders blotted blue as soggy lilacs
With lichen and cloud shadow? It's all free:
So dive a palm down into warm valleys
Of cushion, sift through crumbs, lint, old snacks.
Ore shed by decades of simple couch life:
Dental floss, Scrabble vowels, such nostalgia!
Monopoly hat, racy red brassiere,
Condom wrapper, super ball, pocketknife;
Star Wars action figure (a lost Jawa),
A fist of loose change, enough for a beer,
Proof that nothing in life gets very far:
The mother lode, an unopened Mars bar.

Epitaphs

Suggestions, to be incised on my gravestone

I have gone. Don't be vexed.
You mourn, but you may be next.

Move on, enjoy the day.
I'd love to, but I must stay.

You may think I watch you.
I've got too much to do.

Come. Sit down. Stay a while.
You can't tell, but I smile.

I may have left no clue.
Don't cry. I miss you too.

Like sunlight on the grass,
We move slowly and pass.

Don't linger. Life is tough.
I'll see you soon enough.

She Discovers an Unsent E-Mail to an Ex-Boyfriend

I'm sorry I left you that day at MoMA.
I could at least have tugged your shoulder
Or claimed I went in search of a bathroom.
Your dense jabber put me in a coma.
Your idle pace left me feeling older,
And wherever I stood I felt you loom.
Your thoughts on design from some class you had
And your cribs straight from the museum guide
Didn't work the trick you've come to expect.
I wasn't impressed. In fact, I was sad
When I realized you really have to hide
Yourself with gimmicks I've learned to detect.
It seems nothing in life is worth the pain
Of love, except love. Still, I will abstain.

Guide to the Modern Man (*Beach Issue!*)

Despite valiant headlines to such effect,
What the hell could *GQ*, *Stuff*, or *Esquire*
Know of big topics like "The Modern Man"?
Do they know, really, that he needs respect,
Real-life models to which he might aspire?
A man needs more than watches and sedans.
Skim their pages when you want to know
About cufflinks, dates, and trouser pleats, stag
Nights and sit-ups, cures for back hair and plaque.
We may splash, sport, and flirt in the shallows,
But it is in the depths, off the cold drag
Of continental shelves dropped into black,
Where we are forced, finally, to survive,
Drift, flow and struggle, kick, sink, and then dive.

The Otherwise Sedentary Novelist Finds His Fantasy Turns Out All Wrong

Her ass was just as hard as Formica.
Her knuckles in his side were like rock drills.
This wasn't turning out to be much fun.
Still, he'd come so far. There's nothing like a
No-frills kick, but these were not even "thrills"
In the conventional sense of the term.
"When you try kickboxing down at the Y,
Best not to go home with your instructor,
Unless you are fond of that sort of action.
She's so much fitter, she can't help but pry
Your joints, knead your guts, rattle your 'clever'
Brains to pulp, your kidneys to gelatin.
This scene was such a sweet simple caper,
And painless, when it was still on paper."

The King Issues His Annual Report

I take full responsibility for what happened at Enron.
But saying that, I know in my mind that I did nothing criminal.
—Kenneth Lay

There are worlds I never planned to conquer,

But found myself inflamed by providence.

My famed armies topple your town's tower.

My great ballistae knock you hard on your

Ass. My knights shit on bed and altar, hence

My glory is accomplished. You cower

As well, I see. No surprise there. You know

My works and feats, racks of birds, fame-deep gold

From far countries, my myriad scions:

Friend of Charlemagne, deft with sword and bow.

Yes, you may pay tribute, kneel, and behold.

I'll bed your daughters, behead your peons.

Stupor mundi, one of a kind, my works stun

The world, and it's all so much *goddamned fun.*

Small Consolations

What they call History
is nothing to vaunt of,

being made, as it is,
by the criminal in us:
goodness is timeless.

—W.H. Auden

Song

A song for those who learn forgotten, slow
Skills, crafts submerged long past by massed commerce,
By hard, dark, oily machines, and the din
Of duplicates shipped by the millions, stowed
In cavernous depots to be dispersed
To each home, used once, and then binned.
This is for those who weave by hand, who brew
Their own suds, and roll their own smokes, hammer
Together shelves, print on presses, plant gardens
In vacant lots, raise beams, fire pots, the few
Who challenge the swift, transient tenor
Of the age, the lonely sincere wardens,
The last, noble pull of old ways restored,
Valued and unwanted, admired and ignored.

Symmetries

Love, when mingled with doubt, runs much quicker,
And despair rivals delight at each turn.
The sudden bled juices of early May
Add thrills to life. Such persuasive liquor,
When dried on the wick, primes it to burn.
Something tugs night up like a sheet from day.
Bacchus, with a six-pack, comes for Sibyl,
And the hermit misses the city's strife.
We blank out one future each time we decide.
The fulcrum of time demands so little:
Only that we give some portion of life
To love, or surely we have already died.
Death balances love on scales; goes up, then
What raises it pulls it back down again.

Letter to a Godson

For Christian

Kernel of light sheltered in earth's dark loam,
You were born as the sun skimmed our summer,
And will rise up in time to greet the sky.
You'll claim the world, its noon and night, for home,
And though age pulls horizons like thunder,
Its cold-shadowed rain remains far away.
Who can guess what strange futures you will know,
What roads you will cruise, what odd styles you'll wear;
But the ranges you scale will become yours,
And we'll be slowly left behind, as by a road
When a car speeds off, headed for somewhere
We cannot even imagine as ours.
For now, we know: you'll be tall and quite smart,
Filled with lightning, and summers, from the start.

Love Poem

My love, we know how species run extinct,
And greenest plants grow to fossils in time,
Mountains go molten and run to the sea,
That our careful ideas, all we think,
Will be forgotten, that continents climb
And drop, shift away, collide endlessly;
My love, we know the universe must bend
Until it ends, entropy will labor
Until all is cold and flat, that stars close
Across icy gulfs, suns crash. All things end.
Do not wish our love could last forever,
Or grieve that it is one more thing we lose,
Only that we drive through the dark weather,
Through the gray, through night, and end together.

Literature and Related Embarrassments

Books and harlots have their quarrels in public.

—*Walter Benjamin*

One finds there is time, after all, to wind the clock.
Yet no one noticed it had stopped.

—*John Ashbery*

Meet and Greet

For some, ardent reading forms its own end,
A drawn-out, lonely, unpaid profession.
Even as pastime, it's viewed as creepy.
The mind greets ghosts, and no good to pretend
You'll get much respect. It's not even fun
Most of the time. The classics aren't easy.
This is why you will find literary
Types are either phonies or psychopaths.
Try to ditch the former. Trust the latter.
The true readers know that it's quite scary:
All the hours spent alone, lost in the past.
They survive waves of prattle and patter.
They have learned how little is to be gained
From bragging of all the worlds they've sustained.

Literary Artifacts

Samuel Johnson's gallstone was
"about the size of a pigeon's egg."
(Compare the size of Pepys's!)
—*Richard Altick,* The Scholar Adventurers

Samuel Pepys suffered from a grand gallstone.

Some claim it was fat as a tennis ball.

He had it removed and placed on display

For visitors, and would freely postpone

A tale of war, plague, or great fire to tell

Readers that he had wet himself that day.

Years kept his keepsake but left the journals.

We may never discover Shakespeare's notes

For *Hamlet*, or Byron's burned memoir,

But an orb so solid, perhaps eternal,

Would be a great find. Though missing, one hopes

Something so large can't have gotten too far,

That if we can't name the man from Porlock,

We may still unearth Pepys's famous rock.

Leander Without Heroes

It's hard growing older as a writer.
Poets remain "young" until they're forty!
But "young novelists" are off the menu
By "three O". You begin to scan other
Authors' bios for their dates of birth, stay
Calm and rank yourself up, and know they too
Will learn: as birthdays pass, so do the death
Dates of great and good gone down in their day.
At twenty-five, there goes Mr. John Keats,
So you raise a foaming glass to your health,
And at thirty you rudely lose Shelley
Sodden on sand, victim of his own feats,
Then you're Byron, on the Hellespont, torn,
Not sure you can swim a lap with the storm.

Rules of Order

Elder statesman, for his enemy

"I've no magic. Your witch-hunt won't work.
Some will cower from a well-aimed tag:
Spy, fascist, racist, sexist, to begin;
Wacko, leftist, Nazi, just pull the cork
On some worked-up gasbag and watch the wag
Of mutt and tail alike, as vile terms spin
A frank debate into inquisition.
Sticks and stones, they leave you busted and sore,
But a bad name will plague you a long time.
The first impulse is to hurl them back, then
Duck as they return. But don't. What is more,
Live in hope we might trade ideas, not slime.
Endless battle may be our destiny.
But the world must still hold both you and me."

In the Arena

For his friends

"It's hard to battle someone with no brain,
Hopeless to fight one with no memory,
Pointless to show proof when a mind's made up.
One dumb remark can fill you with disdain,
But you must still respect your enemy.
Stand steady. Don't leave the outcome to luck.
Some fights are worth all the anger they cause.
Not everything is 'just your opinion.'
If that's true, then nothing is worth a damn.
Some discard rules, others cling hard to laws.
Some will dodge, duck, parry, or simply run.
You must expose frauds, cast light, disperse shams.
There may be more than just one right answer,
But there are still some wrong ones, remember."

Decisive Victories

Dream of both marshal and author the same,
One big battle to end it, one big book:
Cannae, Austerlitz, *Don Juan*, *War and Peace*,
Pearl Harbor, *Don Quixote*, final claim
On the age, at least for those who mistook
A Pyrrhic triumph for the Golden Fleece;
A day's win for the campaign; one novel
For the "voice of a whole generation."
Hannibal seized his day, but failed at last,
Troubled down like Fitzgerald, Poe, and Melville.
You can grab for praise, for prime position,
But praise and glory simmer away fast.
And yet, though he pissed it all away, Byron
Still intrigues us, as does Napoleon.

The War Correspondent
Returns to His Neighborhood

Summertime, I hear gunshots from the street.
The windows of my narrow apartment
Are open for lack of a working AC.
Sometimes hoarse threats and fast steps will precede
The quick sharp cracks (*nice trade for such cheap rent*).
Other times shots bring surprise misery
From silence. I dim the lights and raise Bach,
Go back to my book. It is like thunder
On a clear day, or Black Cats popping off
When the Fourth is a month away. The shock
Has worn off, lost all its vagrant wonder,
Even as a man dies screaming in the next lot.
Who can write of such things as become clear
And sane because they are so painfully near?

Thoughts upon Reading
George Gissing's *New Grub Street*

Avoid creditors but court your editors.
A lukewarm notice in the *Times* is like
Heroin and sex combined, remember.
Bring extra pens and aspirin for your tours,
And scan the weekly lists for that fleeting spike
That transmutes memoirs to legal tender.
Go hungry before selling off your books.
The hard times will come and probably stay.
Swim the infested waters where careerists
Circle with their finny tribe—riding old flukes—
Who look famous on paper, who can sway
A committee, while scholars gather interest.
Bored, *natch*, the rest of the world looks on,
While we trawl battlefields to learn who won.

Elegies and Laments

Myn is the ruyne of the hye halles,
The fallynge of the toures and of the walles.

—*Geoffrey Chaucer,* "*The Knight's Tale*"

At the Grave of Thomas Eakins, Late Winter

Woodland Cemetery, Philadelphia

The first visit I failed to find it, where
Commodores and captains lie in brazen
White vaults over humble Quaker enclaves.
Five deer flashed in sun-streaked shade and paused there,
Pure as stone in faint sun flicker, frozen,
And then they dashed and leapt over worn graves.
My formal heart, numb and flawed, was struck raw
To learn life dies in art, yet such stillness
Can stir so fast it seems to disappear:
Time shown in a surgeon's blood-shadowed saw
Or summer's swift rowers slipping from us,
While upriver, to others, they grow nearer.
Wind rearranges sunlight through the pines,
Sowing and destroying endless designs.

Biglin Brothers Racing

Thomas Eakins

Nimble rowers, their art ancient as war,
Raise their oars and ride gently on dented gold
As sun shocks the river to ribboned fire.
They haul hard and halt. Nothing prepares for
Their clear and precise aim. They raise and fold
Their blades under, pull, draw, rest, and respire.
Simple flexed machines of doused oar, bright fleck,
Trained across cold surfaces brisk as steel,
Delicate insect thrash, more than just life,
More than we allow ourselves to expect;
Polished slender shell of lacquered teal
Thrust through late noon light, fine as a knife.
Muscled rowers glide on their mirrored sky,
Winners, a day's champions, built to die.

The Ancient Sailor Leaves
His Heartless Patrician Lover to Her Lyre

You moved against me like a new ocean,
Beautiful—terrifying, and violent.
You thrashed me for nights with your stinging waves.
Like sand I dwindled and came loose; and then
Your cruel music left its audience bent
And wrecked with notes cut onto frost-flashed staves.
I was a small ember you blew to flame.
Now I'm stretched across an acre of bones,
Supine and dizzy in a far inlet.
A cold splendor will burn others the same.
You clout your ice against my cliffs and stones.
You strike my darkness with endless sunset.
Your tempo crashes and pounds the dead land.
Your song haunts me, and it can never end.

Nightmare

Daring and sullen, she tows the world
From beneath me. She stalks, glossed slick with blood;
She spins me blindfolded, drunk, and trips me.
I am haunted by winds that arrive curled
Behind her. She drags a dark, winter flood.
I am dripping and infected, afraid.
There is something behind me, dead, remote;
There is something before me, icy, astral;
I lack the health to get away and home.
She sows storms and tombs. I pull a wet coat
Over my head, twist into a dismal
Crouch. I am sunk beneath drizzle and foam.
She wracks me to skies and depths of fear,
Lit up against the dark and leaning near.

Lines on the Winter Solstice

She hacks another rank of white powder.
My mind sizzles with fallen star-frost.
The drink in my hand changes with a blink.
Everyone chatters. Music gets louder.
Exalted and spent, jagged and time-tossed,
My ruined mind spools across its cracked rink.
My throat is raw and numb. So are my eyes.
My crotch tingles with bitter phosphorous,
Cold drained whorl of ruthless spider longings.
Bottles, dust, and debris cram this dim sty,
Where each light stings, spins down to envious
Shadow, a place hidden from all dawnings.
Lethal hunger driven to narcotic feast,
I feed my center, this bright sleepless beast.

In Bed for a Week

It happens to us all, at least one time,
The black, caught knot of storm threatens, distant,
But buckling closer, waves capped and blown white.
Heavy tides, laden with fresh wreckage, climb,
Drop down the throat; life is a persistent
Ache of sunken vessels and squandered light.
Barrier islands and breakwaters lost,
The sea flails the darkness, its frayed currents,
Wind-flung sediment, shards like stones thrown,
Pooled mirrors blown to blur down the cold coast,
Leaving foam, crushed scum, marsh sun, a grim sense
Of many inherited contours gone.
But the dark flush in the heart will subside,
Drain slowly, slowly draw back as a tide.

Calavera for a Friend

Día de los Muertos

When your heart is scorched out, the unruly world
Will seal around you as a dark ocean
Behind a ship at dusk—the wake will fade
And spread wider, until fully unfurled.
Love reserved for you will slacken. Your portion
Of commerce ends with the last deal you made.
A stranger will take your job, buy your home,
Maybe wear your shirts and shoes, and the books
You cherished will be thumbed by new readers.
Young tourists will roam everywhere you roamed.
Some small items might remain, artifacts,
Footnotes, fingerprints, cuff links, little anchors,
Small burrs that cling: initials carved in a tree,
Your name inscribed where no one will see.

Ernest Hilbert is the editor of the *Contemporary Poetry Review*. He was educated at Oxford University, where he edited the *Oxford Quarterly*. He later became the poetry editor for Random House's magazine *Bold Type* in New York City. He is an antiquarian book dealer in Philadelphia, where he lives with his wife, an archaeologist.

Printed in the USA
CPSIA information can be obtained
at www.ICGtesting.com
JSHW022149150324
59315JS00005B/270

9 781597 093613